TEEN LIFE™

FREQUENTLY ASKED QUESTIONS ABOUT

Sports Injuries

Kathy Furgang

ROSEN
PUBLISHING®

New York

Published in 2008 by The Rosen Publishing Group, Inc.
29 East 21st Street, New York, NY 10010

Library of Congress Cataloging-in-Publication Data

Furgang, Kathy.
Frequently asked questions about sports injuries / Kathy Furgang.
    p.cm.—(FAQ: Teen Life)
Includes bibliographical references and index.
ISBN-13: 978-1-4042-1933-5
ISBN-10: 1-4042-1933-1
1. Sports injuries—Juvenile literature. 2. Sports injuries in children—Juvenile literature.
I. Title.
RD97.F87 2008
617.1'027–dc22

2007001108

Manufactured in the United States of America

Contents

Introduction

Sports can be an important part of staying healthy. If you participate in sports, injuries should be a concern for you. A sports injury can cause any athlete to have trouble playing her favorite game for years to come. Some of the worst sports injuries may even prevent the athlete from competing ever again.

According to Children's Hospital Boston, about thirty million children and teens take part in organized sports. Among these athletes, about three million injuries occur each year. In fact, soccer alone sends more than 100,000 kids to the emergency room every year, reports a study published in the February 2007 issue of *The American Journal of Sports Medicine*. Almost one-third of *all* injuries experienced during childhood are sports-related.

A sports injury can be anything from a bruise or cut to a broken bone or head injury. Sports injuries can be caused by accidents while playing a game, by improper or inadequate stretching or warming up, by using incorrect equipment, or by not playing the game properly. It is important for athletes to admit when they are injured. When athletes deny that they are hurt or suffering, or when they convince themselves that they can "play through the pain," injuries can become even worse.

Members of a soccer team help an injured teammate off the field.

There are ways to stay safe while playing sports, however. Following your coaches' advice, wearing the proper equipment, respecting other players, and playing according to the rules of the game all help to prevent injury. With a little knowledge about how to stay safe, you can have a lifelong love for sports and fitness and remain healthy and active.

one

WHAT ARE SOME COMMON SPORTS INJURIES?

The most common sports injuries include those to the ankle, knee, elbow, shoulder, and neck. These are all places on the body where bones meet bones, and muscles are connected to other muscles. In fact, the knee is one of the body parts that an athlete most commonly injures. It bears a lot of weight and is almost constantly pivoting, maneuvering, stopping, and starting suddenly.

Surrounding your body's bones are connective tissues called ligaments. Muscles are the tissues that help you move your body parts. You use muscles to make any movement, including kicking, throwing, and running. Tissues that connect muscles to bone are called tendons. Muscles, tendons, and ligaments are commonly injured in sports.

Some injuries are less serious than others. Some require little more than rest, while others may require surgery and leave the athlete prone to further injury in the future.

This teenage athlete has sprained her ankle and must walk with crutches.

Common Sports Injuries

There are many ways an athlete can be injured. Here are some common sports injuries, how they are treated, and how to prevent them.

Sprains and Strains

Sprains and strains are the most common sports injuries. A stretch or tear in a ligament is called a sprain. A sprain can be caused by a fall or by the body being hit. Knees, wrists, and ankles are the most common areas of the body that become sprained. Signs of a sprain include pain, swelling, bruising, or inability to move the affected area. If you think you have a sprain, let a coach or other adult know immediately. Do not try to walk with a sprained knee or ankle. Have someone call for help while you sit, and don't put weight on the injured body part until you have been examined.

If you tear, pull, or twist a tendon or muscle, you may have a strain. While you probably know the importance of stretching, some strains are actually caused by overstretching muscles or tendons. This does not mean you should not stretch, however. Make sure you stretch properly before a game or practice so that your muscles are warmed up. One sign of a strain is a muscle spasm, or sudden contraction of a muscle that you cannot control. Other signs are pain and weakness in the muscle or tendon. Some strains are minor, and others are more severe. If major strains are not treated, they can become much more painful.

Major sprains can cause difficulties for athletes. For example, even after sprained ankles heal, many athletes use ankle braces to prevent additional injury and to keep the ankle from moving beyond the normal range of motion. A knee sprain can keep an athlete from participating in sports for many weeks. It can take several weeks for it to heal properly. You must rest a sprain until there is no longer any pain when you move.

Four major ligaments support the knee and allow it to move. These ligaments are the anterior cruciate ligament (ACL), the posterior cruciate ligament (PCL), the medial collateral ligament (MCL), and the lateral collateral ligament (LCL). An injury to any of these ligaments can keep an athlete from participating in her sport for several weeks. A common way to sustain a knee injury is to twist the knee while slipping or moving, or to be hit in the knee or leg. Runners get knee injuries from running too hard or from not warming up properly. Simply overusing the knee can also cause damage to one of the four major ligaments.

Shin Splints

The shin is the front section of your lower leg. Shin splints are overuse injuries—that is, no single event causes them. Instead, they develop slowly from weeks, months, or years of activity that has gradually weakened or irritated the area. Shin splints are pain caused by an inflammation of the tissues that connect to the shinbone. Runners and dancers are most often affected by shin splints. The shin tissues can become overused and inflamed if you run too much, or if you run without warming up properly.

Runners, such as this cross-country runner, often suffer from shin splints because they run so frequently and for long periods of time.

Some people are more prone to shin splints than others. If your feet have an unusually flat or high arch, you are more likely to develop shin splints. If your knees do not align with each other, you may also get more shin splits than other people.

You might have shin splints if you have pain just behind your shins. The pain starts about two-thirds of the way down from your knee. If you feel these pains, tell your coach or doctor. Do not continue exercising at the same rate as before. You may also need to replace your sneakers because their shock absorbency has decreased. Shin splints heal with rest. The length of healing time depends on the severity of the shin splints. Don't resume playing your sport until you have no pain at all when you jog or run.

Dislocation

Your body's bones meet to form joints. When an injury occurs, bones can become separated from each other. When this happens, the joint becomes dislocated. Sports in which dislocations are common include contact sports such as football and soccer, and those that require a lot of stretching or falling to the ground.

Dislocations are emergencies that need hospital treatment as soon as possible. A person with a dislocated joint is in a lot of pain. The tendons surrounding the area stretch, and the longer the patient goes without treatment, the more difficult it is to put the bones back together. The most commonly dislocated joints are in the hand and shoulder.

People who have had dislocations are often left with lasting problems associated with the injury. Athletes must be very careful not to damage the joint again. Even so, there is a chance that the joint will dislocate again, sometimes years later. Dislocations can become a chronic or long-lasting problem for many. Surgery is an option for people who have continual problems with dislocation. The surgery can fuse the joints together so that it is much more difficult for them to become dislocated.

Tennis Elbow, Pitcher's Elbow, and Little League Elbow

Athletes who overuse their arms can experience elbow injuries, which usually develop over time. The most common elbow injuries are tennis elbow, pitcher's elbow, and Little League elbow. Tennis elbow is an inflammation of the bony knob on the outside of the elbow. (Golfer's elbow, a similar injury, affects the inside of the elbow.) Pitcher's elbow is caused by a tendon that becomes inflamed. Besides baseball and softball pitchers, it can affect golfers, rowers, and tennis players. Little League elbow affects baseball and softball players, and is caused by a repetitive thrusting of the arm in an over-hand motion. The motion damages the elbow and the shoulder to some degree. Preteen and teenage athletes have a greater risk of injury, since they are still growing. Signs of Little League elbow include a weakened, painful elbow, especially when pitching. Doctors warn that throwing more than 300 pitches a week (at practices, as well as games) can be a danger to growing athletes' elbow joints, muscles, and tendons.

If you experience any elbow, arm, or wrist pain while playing any of these sports, stop and see a doctor. The injury can be treated with ice, rest, mild pain medicine, or an arm brace. The injury can become very painful if it is ignored and may need surgery.

Tennis elbow occurs with repetitive grasping and squeezing that over-exercises the elbow and causes its tendons to become painful and inflamed.

Concussion

A concussion is temporary unconsciousness caused by a blow to the head. Sports that have a higher risk for concussion include boxing, football, and soccer. However, any sport that uses a ball, or any contact or team sport where there is the possibility of a collision, could potentially cause a concussion. When the head is hit hard, the brain is jarred inside the skull. The blow to the head might be straight on, or it might twist the neck and head. These twisting blows are most likely to cause unconsciousness and may result in neck injuries. An athlete might be unconscious for a few seconds to several minutes. Many have no memory of events directly before or after their concussion. Concussions can cause bleeding in the brain, which is a serious condition that needs immediate attention.

Signs of a concussion include nausea, vomiting, uneven dilation of the pupils, headache, dizziness and loss of balance. Another sign is involuntary body convulsion, similar to a seizure. Also look for signs of confusion or memory loss. The most serious result of a concussion is coma, in which a person cannot wake from unconsciousness.

To prevent concussion, wear your helmet when participating in sports. (It is also important that the helmet fit properly, since wearing equipment that doesn't fit correctly can lead to inadequate safety protection and injury.) Biking, football, baseball, and other sports require hard helmets that can help to prevent a blow to the head. Although death from a sports injury is rare, the leading cause of these deaths is from brain injury. Of all the brain

The risk of concussion in boxing is very high, and can result in lasting brain damage. Other contact sports such as football and hockey are also leading causes of concussion.

injuries among American children and adolescents, about 21 percent occurred as a result of sports injuries (the majority of which occurred in skateboarding, skating, and cycling incidents).

Once an athlete has suffered a concussion, his chances of permanent brain injury become greater if he endures more concussions in the future. This is why boxing becomes increasingly dangerous for athletes who have been repeatedly knocked out.

Achilles Tendon Injuries

The Achilles tendon is located at the back of the heel. It is the largest tendon in the body. It can withstand a lot of pressure from jumping and running, but it is the most frequently injured tendon. When the Achilles tendon is overused, it becomes damaged and inflamed. If you increase the amount that you run or the speed at which you run, add stairs or hills to your workout too quickly, run and stop rapidly and repeatedly as in soccer or tennis, or overdo your exercise routine, you may have trouble with your Achilles tendon.

Symptoms of Achilles tendonitis include minor pain after exercise that increases with time, stiffness, swelling, or slowness in the leg. If you experience any of these symptoms, see a doctor. Recommended treatment may include total rest from exercise, or switching to an exercise that does not produce stress on the Achilles. The injury may need to be bandaged. It may also require stretching, massage, or medication. If these treatments do not work, surgery to repair the tendon may be a last resort. Recovery from such a surgery is slow and requires a cast to limit movement.

To prevent Achilles tendonitis, make sure your sneakers are in good condition and provide a cushion for your heel. Wear footwear that is designed for the particular activity in which you are participating; improper footwear can lead to injury. Stretch and warm up properly before exercising. Be sure to stretch your heels and calves. Gradually increase your workouts so that you do not work your body too hard at once. Do not strain too much if you are not accustomed to it. Overstressing yourself will result in injuries, and you will not be able to participate in your sport until you have healed.

Growth Plate Injuries

Children and adolescents have growth plates—areas of growing tissue near each end of the long bones (bones that are longer than they are wide). You have growth plates at your fingers, forearms, collarbone, hips, knees, ankles, and feet. Sometime in your teens, these areas, which determine the length and shape of the mature bone, close and are replaced by solid bone. Until this happens, however, your growth plates will be susceptible to fracture because they are the weakest areas of your growing skeleton. Approximately half of all growth plate injuries occur at the wrist, but they also occur frequently in the lower bones of the leg. According to the National Institute of Arthritis and Musculoskeletal and Skin Diseases (NIAMS), growth plate injuries occur twice as often in boys as in girls. The greatest incidence is among fourteen- to sixteen-year-old boys and eleven- to thirteen-year-old girls.

If you have pain anywhere you have a growth plate, describe the pain to your doctor. Treatment depends on the type, location, and extent of the fracture, but can include immobilizing the injury in a cast or splint, surgery, and strengthening exercises. Easing back into your sports routine after you have healed can help you from reinjuring yourself.

Ten Great Questions to Ask When You're Asking for Help

1 Will I have to stop playing this sport?

2 How long do I have to rest or not play the game?

3 Will this injury affect how I play other sports?

4 What should I do if my coach pressures me to start playing again before I'm ready?

5 Can I play again if my injury starts to feel better, even if I've only been healing for a little while?

6 If I have to take pain medication, could I become addicted to it?

7 What if this same injury happens again?

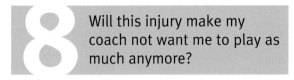

8 Will this injury make my coach not want me to play as much anymore?

9 What should I do if the pain does not go away?

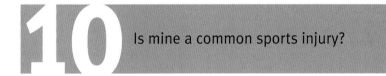

10 Is mine a common sports injury?

R.I.C.E. Method

Remembering **R.I.C.E.** is useful in the treatment of sports injuries. The acronym stands for the four things you can do to improve your injury and continue on the road to healing:

- **Rest.** Do not follow your regular exercise or sports routine after you have been injured. Give your body some rest. Your doctor can tell you how much time it will take for your particular injury to heal, but recovery from most injuries requires that the person be patient so as not to cause further aggravation.
- **Ice.** When you are first injured, apply ice to the affected area. Ice packs can be used in twenty-minute intervals (leave ice on the injury for twenty minutes, then take it off for twenty minutes), up to eight times a day. If no ice packs

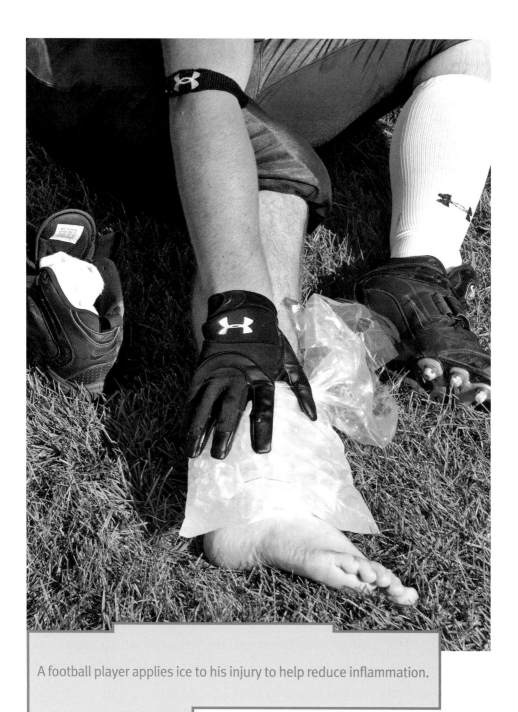

A football player applies ice to his injury to help reduce inflammation.

are available, wrap ice in a towel or cloth. Do not apply ice directly to your skin—it can cause frostbite. Do not apply heat to the area during the first day or two of the injury. This may increase swelling instead of reducing it.

➤ **Compression.** Wrapping the affected area with bandages, elastic wraps, or splints will compress the injury. This can help to reduce swelling. Ask a doctor or nurse what kind of compression might be right for your kind of injury. Do not make the decision on your own. Incorrectly wrapping the injury or applying splints improperly can make the injury worse.

➤ **Elevation.** To keep swelling down, try to elevate the affected area on a pillow. Sit so that the injury is above the level of your heart.

WHAT IF I BREAK A BONE?

Bones are tough and will bend under strain. If the pressure is too much or too sudden, however, your bones can be damaged. A fracture, which is a break in a bone, can occur when there is sudden impact on the bone. A break can be clean and simple and not come through the skin. If it does come through the skin, it is known as a compound fracture and has a higher risk of infection.

Bone fractures are very painful. A compound fracture can be identified easily if the bone is sticking through the skin. A simple fracture can be harder to identify, since you can't see the broken bone. Simple fractures can only be identified with an X-ray. So if you think you may have a broken bone but are not sure, do not move your affected limb or body part. Remain still and call for help. If the bone is not broken, your injury may end up being a sprain.

A patient has a cast on her broken leg. Fractures can take a few weeks to several months to heal, depending on the extent of the injury.

Treating a Broken Bone

An amazing thing about bones is that they are designed to heal themselves. However, a doctor needs to reset the bone, or fit the broken pieces back together. The realigned bone then will be stabilized by a cast or splint. Once it has been reset, a broken or fractured bone will start to reknit its cells and become whole again. The top layer usually grows over the break first, smoothing out the seams, and is followed by the tough, bony matter underneath.

More complicated fractures may require surgery. The bone will be put back together internally with metal pieces called pins. These fractures may take longer to heal, and the patient may be immobilized for months.

Protecting the Injury

There are several ways doctors keep the pieces of bone still so that the bone can mend itself without being knocked out of place.

Casts and Splints

Casts are made of plaster and are very hard so that the broken bone cannot shift or move. Typically, a cast is used on a simple fracture that will easily heal if it is just kept still. Besides keeping the body part absolutely still, the cast adds enough weight to stimulate bone cell regrowth. Splints are not as strong as casts, but they also keep the bone from moving.

Cast Braces

Cast braces are casts used for leg breaks that will heal properly, even when the knee is allowed to move a little. They come in two parts—one piece for above the knee, and one for below. Before the plaster dries, a flexible joint is placed between the sections so that the patient can bend his or her knee.

Traction

If a bone breaks and isn't used again, often it will never heal. Bones need constant pressure and use in order to signal the body to regenerate. If a patient is bedridden after an injury, frequently he or she will be put in traction. A plaster cast is attached to a pulley system that exerts steady force on the break, stimulating the bone to mend itself.

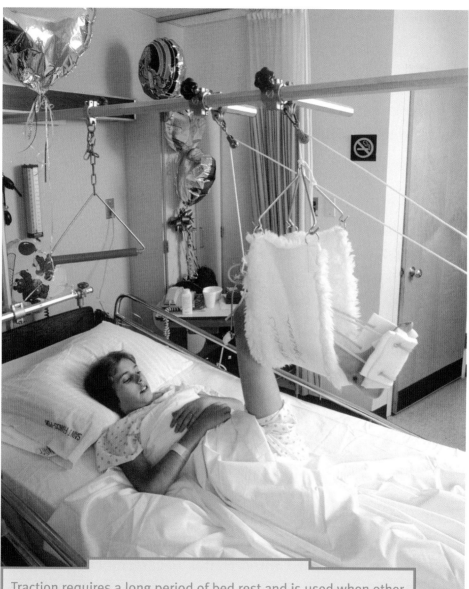

Traction requires a long period of bed rest and is used when other treatment options, including surgery, are not possible. Traction involves the use of a gentle, steady pulling action to align bone fragments.

External Fixation

This type of setting requires pins to be run through the bone parts and then secured to a thin metal piece, or frame, that remains outside the body. Doctors have to use an external fixation when the break will not heal properly just by keeping the area still, such as with a cast.

Internal Fixation

Internal fixation is used when a bone is crushed into many pieces, or the break is so severe that external fixation is not sufficient to keep everything aligned so that it will heal properly. Sometimes doctors insert long screws through parts of bone, securing bones to one another. In another configuration, a metal plate is attached to the outside of the bone. Screws are drilled through the broken pieces and attached to the plate, which keeps the bone in the right formation as it heals. At other times, doctors stick a metal rod down the center of a long broken bone, then screw the broken pieces of bone to the pin in the center. Once the bone is healed, the pins stay inside the patient.

And Finally . . . Superglue?

Since superglue works on almost anything, why not use it on bones? Doctors in the United States occasionally use a fast-drying liquid cement to help bind broken bones that might otherwise take weeks to heal on their own. For example, if you fracture your heel bone, a doctor might glue the small bones back together. The glue keeps the parts of bone together.

When they are together, new bone growth is stimulated and healing occurs.

Possible Complications

If a patient is not treated for a complex fracture quickly, blood loss is a danger. Later problems may include slowed growth in a child or teen who has had a fracture and has not yet finished growing. If the break occurs close to a joint where much growing is done, the fracture may cause future growth to be slowed down.

Most casts are kept on for three to six weeks, and further rest is needed for about a month. Leg bones take longer to heal than other bones. If you are healing from a broken bone, tell your doctor about any swelling, skin discoloration, or loss of movement in your fingers or toes. Also report any pain or numbness. These may be signs that the bone is not healing properly.

Stress Fractures

Another kind of bone fracture, called a stress fracture, happens slowly over time. Athletes who run or jump, including runners, gymnasts, and tennis and basketball players, are especially prone to stress fractures. A stress fracture is caused by a continual, repetitive action. Your muscles usually absorb the shock of repeated action. But if they are too tired or they are not conditioned well enough, they cannot absorb the shock properly. Therefore, the bone will absorb the shock. Over time, the

This radioactive scan shows a stress fracture in an athlete's foot. She felt pain while merely walking.

bone gets tiny breaks in it. These breaks are called stress fractures. More than half of all stress fractures occur in the lower leg. This makes sense when you realize that your lower leg supports the weight of your whole body.

When a stress fracture occurs, you will feel pain. The pain will increase if you keep exercising or playing sports. If you feel a slight pain from repetitive action, immediately slow down. Do not continue at the same pace, or the pain and damage will worsen. Once a doctor has diagnosed a stress fracture, rest is the most effective treatment. Most stress fractures heal themselves within six to eight weeks if the affected area is rested.

The best way to avoid stress fractures is to not overdo your training or workout. A runner cannot run three miles a day without gradually working up to that distance. In addition, pay attention to the equipment you use. In basketball and tennis, for example, switching from a softer court to a harder one takes some adjustment. Take it easy at first. Allow your body time to adapt to jumping, running, and pivoting on the harder surface.

Myths and Facts

About Sports Injuries

Myth

Someone who is injured while playing sports must have done something wrong. Fact ➡ While using proper equipment and following the game's rules can prevent some injuries, not all injuries are avoidable. If you are injured, do not blame yourself or anyone else. Instead, try to understand that accidents are part of the game and that some accidents cannot be prevented.

Myth

Good athletes can play through the pain if they get hurt. Fact ➡ Playing through the pain can make an injury worse. Don't try to be tough and play when you are in pain. Let your coach know as soon as you notice any signs of pain or injury. You will be of more use to your team if you stay well than if you play while hurt and make your injury worse.

Myth

Sports injuries happen more often to older people. Fact ➡ Sports injuries can happen to anyone at any age. Teens and growing children may have more energy than adults, but they also have more fragile bodies. Children and teens are still growing and need extra protection for their growing bones.

It's OK for coaches to get angry with athletes for being injured. Fact ➡ A coach should be supportive and helpful to his or her team. The well-being of an athlete is more important than the team's win/loss record. If you have a coach who gets angry with an athlete because of an injury, he or she should be reported to your school or local sports organization.

Proper shoes are important. If you take these precautions, you may avoid injury altogether and not have to deal with the pain of stress fractures and the time it takes for them to heal.

Vertebrae Injuries

Your vertebrae are a series of bones that make up your backbone, or spinal column. Each vertebra has places where muscles attach, and each has a space through which your spinal cord passes. Your spinal cord is made of crucial nerves that control the movements and sensations in your entire body. Every second of every day, your brain sends messages through your spinal

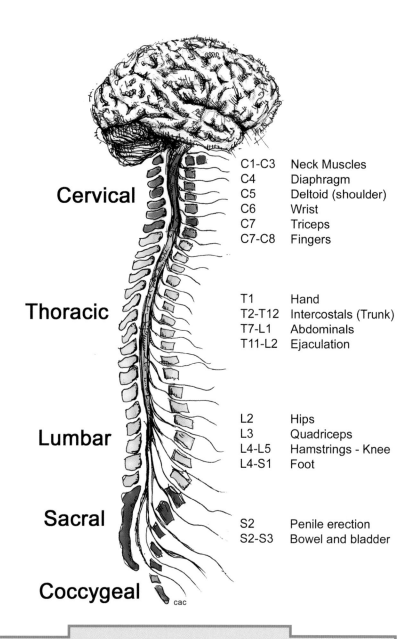

C1-C3	Neck Muscles
C4	Diaphragm
C5	Deltoid (shoulder)
C6	Wrist
C7	Triceps
C7-C8	Fingers
T1	Hand
T2-T12	Intercostals (Trunk)
T7-L1	Abdominals
T11-L2	Ejaculation
L2	Hips
L3	Quadriceps
L4-L5	Hamstrings - Knee
L4-S1	Foot
S2	Penile erection
S2-S3	Bowel and bladder

Cervical

Thoracic

Lumbar

Sacral

Coccygeal

Nerves leave the spinal cord at different levels and control various parts of the body. The extent to which movement and sensation are affected depends on the level of injury. Damage below T1 usually does not involve the arms and hands. Damage above T1, however, involves paralysis of the arms as well as the legs.

cord to areas all around your body. When the vertebrae in your backbone are injured, the spinal cord is usually injured as well.

When playing contact sports such as football, it is possible to sustain a serious injury to one or more of your vertebrae. Other sports, like diving, biking, horseback riding, snow-boarding, and ice-skating, can also cause accidents that affect the vertebrae.

Contact sports can create stress fractures to the vertebrae, which make it very painful and difficult to move, or they can cause actual breaks that affect nerves and tendons. When a small vertebrae break occurs, a surgeon can fuse, or connect, two vertebrae together so that they act as one. The injury and surgery rehabilitation can be painful because of the nerves that are affected.

There are two kinds of spinal cord injuries. A complete spinal injury means that there are no messages coming from the brain to the body parts below the injury. A person with a complete spinal cord injury is paralyzed—that is, he cannot move or feel parts of the body from the point of the injury down. An incomplete spinal injury means that only some messages can be sent from the brain to the body parts below the injury. Someone with an incomplete spinal cord injury has only limited movement and sensation from the point of his injury down.

Broken vertebrae sometimes result in limited damage to the spinal cord. Immediate medical attention is needed for someone who suffers such an injury. There should be no attempt to move the person except by trained medical professionals. Signs of a spinal cord injury include severe pain in the neck, head, or

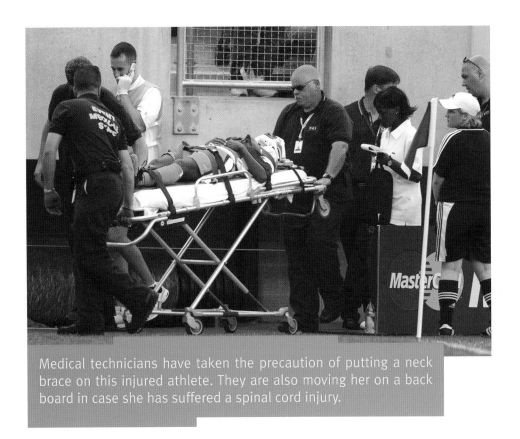

Medical technicians have taken the precaution of putting a neck brace on this injured athlete. They are also moving her on a back board in case she has suffered a spinal cord injury.

back; tingling or numbness in the hands or feet; loss of control over any body part; or odd bumps on the head or backbone.

While breaks to vertebrae can heal with time, spinal cord nerves do not heal themselves. Surgeries are sometimes performed to transplant nerves from other parts of the body into the spinal cord. However, the success rate of spinal cord surgeries is low, and the injury remains a life-changing one.

three

WHO WILL TREAT
MY INJURY?

Your body knows how to react to an injury and how to begin healing itself. The body reacts with pain so that you know right away it's time to stop playing or moving around. The affected area becomes inflamed and swollen so that extra blood can flow to the area. Your blood carries the nutrients your body needs to heal the injury. The damaged tissue begins to be removed by white blood cells and replaced by scar tissue, or tissue that remains after a wound has been healed.

Some injuries are more serious, however, and cannot heal easily on their own. It is then important to seek treatment. You should see a doctor if you feel pain during a game or practice (do not attempt to play through the pain), or if your coach advises that you do so. Talking with your family physician is a good place to start. He or she may also recommend that you see a professional who specializes in treating injuries or specific parts of the body.

Doctors and Other Trained Professionals

There are a number of different kinds of doctors and other trained professionals who treat injuries. A few of them can be contacted if you just want to ask some questions about your exercise habits to make sure you stay injury-free.

Physical Therapist

Physical therapists, or PTS, are trained health professionals who work with people who have suffered accidents or injury, or who need to strengthen their bodies for any other reason. They often work with injured athletes.

Physical therapists use methods that exercise the affected area without adding extra strain to the muscles, joints, or tendons. Some of the treatments they might suggest include therapeutic exercise, cardiovascular endurance training, and heat treatments. For example, whirlpool baths are one way to help a patient practice moving a limb again because the movement of the water keeps pressure off the affected area. It also eliminates the stress of gravity on their bodies. In addition to whirlpools, weights, special bicycles, inflatable stretching balls, and massage are often used in physical therapy.

Many physical therapists have offices in hospitals, and others have private practices. Regardless of where the office is located, it is equipped to treat a wide range of injuries. If a person's injury

A physical therapist helps a patient with exercises that will help improve the patient's arm strength.

is severe and she cannot travel to the therapist's office, the therapist may visit the patient's home.

Physical therapy can last a few weeks, months, or years, depending on the severity of the injury. For example, after a broken arm or leg has healed, you may need to see a physical therapist. If your bone and muscles heal well, the therapist may give you additional exercises to do at home and you will not have to go to the office anymore.

The exercises that you learn in physical therapy can be used years after your injury has healed. Simple stretching exercises

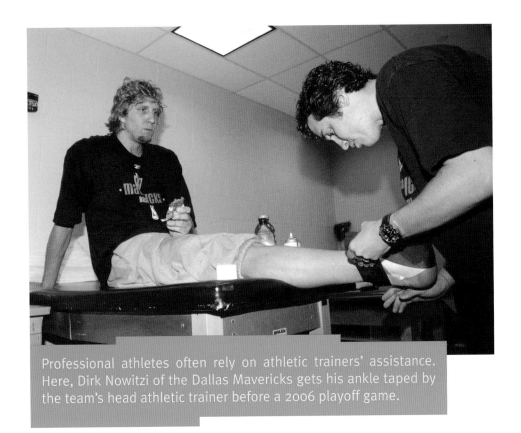

Professional athletes often rely on athletic trainers' assistance. Here, Dirk Nowitzi of the Dallas Mavericks gets his ankle taped by the team's head athletic trainer before a 2006 playoff game.

can help keep a former injury site from being injured again. Athletes have to take special care with the parts of their bodies that were once injured. For example, someone who has suffered from shin splints may have to spend more time and care stretching the leg muscles to avoid the same injury again.

Athletic Trainer

An athletic trainer provides aid to injured athletes. Whether they have muscle cramps or are recovering from time spent in a cast, an athletic trainer is concerned with keeping athletes in their healthiest shape or returning them to health as quickly as possible. Some of an athletic trainers' main goals are to educate athletes on the many ways they can prevent injuries when exercising. They also guide injured athletes through the process of rehabilitation—a process that will hopefully allow them to make a full recovery. Your school may have an athletic trainer on staff who cares for student athletes free of charge.

Massage Therapist

More and more people are becoming patients of massage therapists because they want relief from injuries or because they believe massage will help them deal with the stresses of daily life. A massage can help relieve tension, or "knots" in your muscles, increase circulation through your muscles, and, if done on a regular basis, improve your overall health. Getting a rubdown from a trained professional can also help an athlete recover from tough training and decrease chances of injury. At this time, most doctors will not recommend that you see a massage therapist, but if you ask them for their opinion, most will agree that massages are beneficial to your health.

Kinesiologist

Kinesiology is the science of studying body movement. A kinesiologist's job is to increase the activity level and total well-being of the person he or she is treating. There are many different fields within kinesiology; a practitioner may concentrate on the respiratory system or work to resolve problems with a patient's movement. A kinesiologist who focuses on rehabilitation would perform muscle testing to evaluate any structural, mental, or

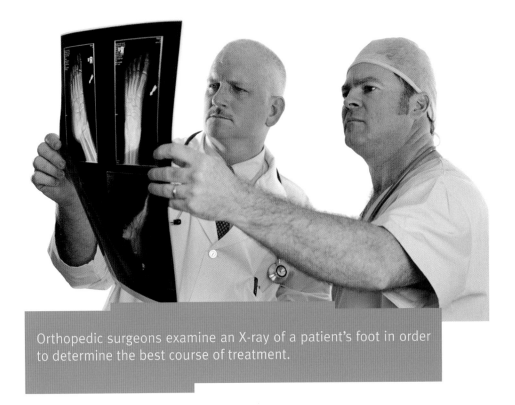

Orthopedic surgeons examine an X-ray of a patient's foot in order to determine the best course of treatment.

nutritional problems that you may have. If you have to see a kinesiologist, you should expect to be evaluated just like you would be by your family doctor. However, a kinesiologist will be looking for movement problems. If he or she finds one, the next step would be to create a rehabilitation program for you.

Orthopedic Surgeon

Orthopedics is the branch of medicine concerned with the musculoskeletal system (involving both the muscular and the skeletal systems). Orthopedic surgeons specialize in diagnosing and treating bones, muscles, joints, ligaments, tendons, and nerves. If you end up needing surgery, a physical therapist will help you afterward to exercise and strengthen the affected area. This will help you heal fully and prevent additional injuries.

Consider Your Options

Each year it seems there are more methods of getting injured athletes quickly back into the game. Some of these methods involve risky surgeries on growing bones and expensive procedures that require a long recovery period. Listen to the advice of your doctor about how to recover from your injury. If your doctor suggests surgery, think about and consider it with your parents, along with all of the other possibilities for recovery. It is up to you and your family to decide how to proceed with an injury. Until you are eighteen and can afford to pay for any procedure yourself, your parents will have a say in your treatment and recovery.

four

HOW DO I COPE WITH THE EFFECTS OF AN INJURY?

Suppose you have been playing sports since you were a small child. You love to play and compete and keep your body in top form. Then you are injured and suddenly out of the game for the season. You are devastated. What can you do? Your team depends on you to help win games. Your coach will be feeling the pressure of you not playing. You keep going over how you got injured in your mind, and you can't believe it happened to you. These are all issues that athletes must deal with if they experience a serious sports injury.

Psychological Effects of an Injury

The psychological effects of sports injuries can have a big impact on athletes. People who can no longer do what they love can become depressed or saddened. They may feel like they are losing out on time with their team, or that someone else may take their place while they are out of the game.

It might be hard to attend games and practices and to watch teammates play while you are stuck on the sidelines. In the long run, however, it might be psychologically helpful for you to support the team and to remain part of the experience. If your doctor allows you to ride on the bus with the team, for example, you could still go to away games with them. Even though you won't be able to play, you'll stay informed about any team news or developments. You also can support your team and cheer them on.

Getting Professional Help

Sports injuries can be severe, and a top athlete may get the news that she will no longer be able to play the game, or play it at the same level. She may no longer be considered for a scholarship, and dreams of playing the sport professionally may be shattered. If this happens to you and you have trouble accepting it, talk to someone about your feelings. Go to a parent, coach, teacher, or other adult that you trust. You can also talk to a counselor or therapist. There are psychologists who specialize in teens and their issues. Or you might find a psychologist who specializes in sports-related issues.

Talking to someone about your feelings, even for a little while, can help you to cope with your situation. People may not realize how much playing the game means to you. You may feel that you were somehow to blame for the injury. You don't know what you will do if you can't play sports. Talking out all of your feelings will help you to cope as your injuries heal.

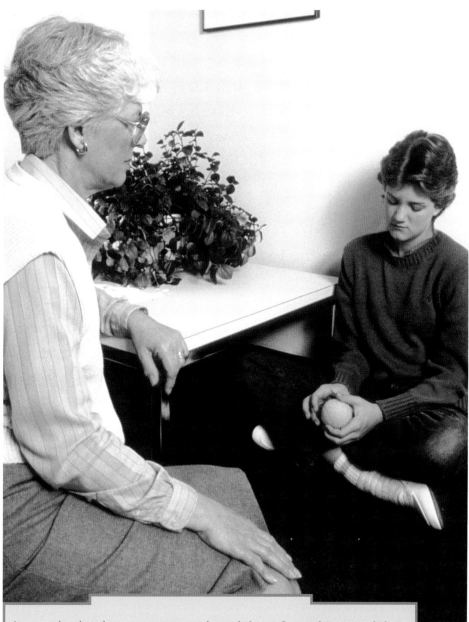

It may be hard to accept a serious injury. Sometimes an injury means that the athlete can no longer play her sport. It can help to talk to a coach, school counselor, or another professional.

Making the Best of Things

A sentence of sitting out the season does not mean a lifetime of sitting on the sidelines. Even athletes who could no longer be considered for professional teams because of serious sports injuries can have a lifetime of enjoying sports and being active. Think about why you enjoy sports in the first place. Think about the fun you have being on the court or field and playing with friends. You do not have to be destined for a life of inactivity. Get advice from your doctor. If he or she says it is OK to participate in other sports, consider trying something new.

If a career in sports is what you always wanted and you can no longer compete on that level, think about related careers. Reporters, photographers, physical therapists, coaches, trainers, umpires, gym teachers, and many others have careers that deal with sports and athletes every day. Ask a guidance counselor or gym teacher for more information about sports careers.

five

HOW CAN I AVOID INJURY?

It is a good idea to talk to your doctor before starting a sport. A physical exam can help spot any problems or weaknesses that might affect your participation or lead to injury. Doctors and coaches have similar advice for avoiding sports injuries in the first place. One important thing is to not put extra stress or strain on your body through sports. Even if you specialize in one sport, it may not be wise to play the same sport all year long. Your body needs a break after each season. Many athletes like to play different sports depending on the season. This works certain parts of the body, while other parts get more rest. For example, a baseball or softball pitcher might need to rest his or her arm at the end of the season. That athlete might choose to bike or play soccer to work on the leg muscles, while resting the arm muscles and joints.

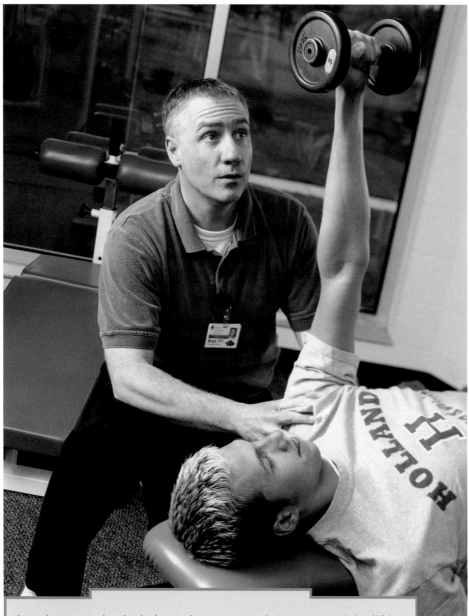

A trainer or physical therapist can teach proper weight-lifting technique. Here, a physical therapist shows his patient how to use free weights.

Avoiding Overuse Injuries

Overuse injuries develop slowly from weeks, months, or years of activity that gradually weakens or irritates the muscles, until exercise eventually becomes difficult or impossible. In many cases, overuse injuries (knee pain, shin splints, and tendonitis are some of the most common of these injuries) could be avoided if people studied technique, got appropriate rest, and used proper equipment when exercising.

Technique

Poor technique—whether during weight lifting, running, cycling, calisthenics, gymnastics, or other physical activity—is a common reason for injury. Get instruction on correct technique before you try any activity for the first time. If you decide that you want to be a cyclist or a mountain biker, for example, it is a good idea to learn the proper riding techniques. If you're using weights, they should be lifted in slow, controlled movements. Never jerk or snap a weight from the floor or its stand. Doing so is a sure way to invite debilitating injuries such as muscle strains or tears. Stretches should also be performed slowly and carefully. Don't twist your knees, and keep your feet as flat as you can. Posture is important as well, especially during strength and flexibility training. In general, keep your back straight, your knees bent, and look directly ahead. Ask trained and knowledgeable instructors to show you correct body positioning for individual exercises.

Warming Up and Cooling Down

Proper, thorough warm-ups and cool-downs before and after practices, games, or competitions are critical to remaining injury-free. Take the time before and after every activity to let your body adjust. You cannot just throw a switch to start or finish a workout. When you do, you are bound to end up injured.

Always warm up before you exercise, no matter what that exercise may be. Warming up is a way to safely make the transition from a state of rest to a state of exertion. By slowly easing into your exercise routine, you give your muscles a chance to stretch. You also increase the blood flow to those muscles, priming them for what's to come. Instead of shocking your body, you gradually build up to the point where it's ready for vigorous exercise. With a good warm-up, you'll drastically reduce your risk of injury.

What are the ingredients of a good warm-up? It depends on what you're planning to do afterward. One of the best ways to warm up is by going on a brisk walk or an easy jog. Five to ten minutes is usually enough to loosen up and bring heat to your joints and muscles. Go slow. Don't push yourself too hard. You want to get your heart rate up, but not too high. If you're out of breath, you're going too fast.

After that short walk or run—you can also use a treadmill if you can't get outside (or you can jump rope, hop up and down, do jumping jacks, etc.)—do a few stretches, focusing on the major muscle groups of your body. Stretch your shoulders, arms, legs, and back. You don't need to push yourself; you just

Stretching is an important part of the warming-up and cooling-down processes. This athlete stretches before she starts her run.

want to feel loose. After these first stretches, you're ready for more intense exercise.

The cool-down is based on the same principles as the warm-up, only in reverse. After exercise, it's good to gradually bring your body back to its natural resting state. Doing so speeds recovery and ultimately results in greater improvements in performance.

During the cool-down period, you reduce the intensity of exercise. After you've finished playing your sport, your muscles are hot and fatigued. Your pulse may be high and your breathing rapid. The goal, then, would be to bring your heart rate to resting levels, slow down your breathing, and cool down your muscles. You don't want to go from a full sprint to standing still. To do so would be just as shocking to your body as rolling out of bed in the morning and immediately sprinting to school.

Start your cool-down by performing the same exercises you had been doing, but at a lower intensity. If you were running hard, take a slow five- to ten-minute jog. Slow down further every couple of minutes, until eventually you reach a walk.

After you finish the easy jogging and walking, follow with some stretching. Again, as with the warm-up, focus on major muscle groups, especially the muscles in your legs, arms, shoulders, and back. This is a great time to improve your flexibility. Because your body is warm after a hard workout, your muscles, tendons, and other connective tissues are easily stretched. By the end of your cool-down, you should feel calm and relaxed.

Professional athletes know the importance of warming up their bodies before intense exercise. Members of Portugal's soccer team stretch prior to the start of a 2006 World Cup match.

In general, any cool-down should include at least ten minutes of very easy exercise and stretching. This so-called "active recovery" period, during which your muscles are working, but only lightly, will aid in the removal of lactic acid (a chemical compound that forms during intense exercise, and which is felt in muscles as a burning sensation) from the blood, return your heart rate and blood pressure to their normal resting levels, lead to better strength and flexibility, and will help prevent injury.

How a "Buddy" Can Help

If you are doing strength training, by far the most important thing you can do to ensure your safety is to always work out with a partner. Your partner is your "buddy." If you need a hand or if something goes wrong, your buddy can help, and you can do the same for that person. Strength training, for example, often involves lifting heavy weights. When you lift, you should always have a spotter. Your buddy can fill this job for you. The spotter stands right next to you as you perform your exercises. When you lift a weight, he or she is ready to help you lower it to the ground if you need assistance.

Role of Coaches and Trainers

Another good way to avoid injuries is to follow the advice of your coaches. Most coaches are trained to spot the signs that someone is tired and could suffer an injury if he continues to

This athlete helps avoid injury by having a "buddy" spot him while he lifts a barbell in his school's weight room.

play without a rest. For example, a coach should be able to recognize when a pitcher looks tired and is not throwing as well as he was previously. It is not the athlete's fault if he is tired. It just means that he must take a rest to avoid injury. The coach should have a plan and can put another pitcher into the game while the other rests. If you are playing a sport and suddenly feel tired, let your coach know.

A coach might be able to improve an athlete's technique to help her avoid injury. For example, a swimming coach can instruct a swimmer on the proper way to hold and use her

Know the rules of the game, and listen to your coach. His or her advice can often help you and your teammates avoid injury.

arms and hands while doing a particular stroke. This can keep the athlete from injuring her shoulders or elbows.

Some teams have a sports trainer to help them. A sports trainer's job is to assist athletes in performing their very best. This includes tips on technique, diet, and getting proper rest. A trainer may help a football team with strength training on weights and other equipment. This training keeps athletes in good shape and helps to prevent them from being injured during practices and games.

A trainer can also teach you how to spot effectively. It is important to keep your knees bent and your eyes on your partner. Communication—both verbal and physical—is crucial as your partner goes through his or her routine.

Supervision by trained adults is crucial to injury prevention. Someone with years of experience in weight training or flexibility training can help spot potentially dangerous situations before anyone gets hurt.

Caution: Don't Overdo It

The human body needs rest as much as it needs food and water. Even professional athletes do not train every day because they know that they must rest to stay strong and fit. However, some athletes get so involved in trying to excel that they push their bodies too far. They don't give themselves enough time to recuperate. Because of this, they develop painful injuries, such as stress fractures and torn muscles, ligaments, tendons, and cartilage.

Make sure to maintain proper perspective, and set realistic goals for yourself based on your age and level of fitness. (Coaches and more experienced athletes can be a great help with this.) Also, pay attention to how your body feels; it will tell you when it needs a rest.

Achilles tendon The body's largest tendon, located in the back of the heel.

acronym A word formed by using the first letter of the words used to create it. (For example, R.I.C.E. stands for Rest, Ice, Compression, Elevation.)

chronic Having a particular long-term illness or condition; always present or recurring.

coma A state of deep unconsciousness caused by injury or illness.

compression The reduction of the size or volume of something by applying pressure, or the act or result of being treated in this way.

concussion Temporary unconsciousness caused by a blow to the head.

continual Happening again and again.

dislocation Separation of two bones that occurs at a joint.

fracture A break in a bone.

frostbite Damage caused to body tissue by prolonged exposure to freezing conditions.

gravity Force that attracts objects toward Earth's surface.

growth plate Places on a child's body where adult bones have not fully formed.

immobilize To keep from moving.

joint The place where two bones fit together.

ligament Connective tissue surrounding bones.

muscles Body tissues that help to move body parts.

orthopedic surgeon Doctor specializing in diagnosing and treating bones, muscles, tendons, ligaments, and nerves.

paralyzed Unable to move the body.

physical therapist Medical professional who helps exercise and strengthen areas of the body that have been injured.

plaster A mixture of water with lime and sand or cement that dries into a hard, smooth surface.

realign To return to a former position.

scar tissue Tissue that remains on the body after a wound has healed.

seizure A sudden onset of uncontrolled movements of the body.

shin splints Pain and inflammation of tissues that surround shins.

splint A strip of rigid material used to keep a broken bone from moving.

sprain A stretch or tear in a ligament.

strain A tear, pull, or twist of a tendon or muscle.

stress fractures Tiny breaks in bones caused by repetitive actions such as running.

tendon Tissue that connects muscles to bone.

tendonitis Irritation or inflammation of a tendon.

unconscious Not in a waking, or conscious, state.

vertebrae The series of small bones that make up the backbone.

American Sports Medicine Institute (ASMI)

2660 10th Avenue South, Suite 505

Birmingham, AL 35205

(205) 918-0000

Web site: http://www.asmi.org

ASMI's mission is to improve the understanding, prevention, and treatment of sports-related injuries through education and research.

HealthFinder

National Health Information Center

P.O. Box 1133

Washington, DC 20013-1133

Web site: http://www.healthfinder.gov

Part of the Department of Health and Human Services, HealthFinder is a guide to reliable health information. Find information on all sorts and injuries, including fractures, Achilles tendonitis, concussion, and Little League elbow.

National Athletic Trainers' Association (NATA)

2952 Stemmons Freeway, #200

Dallas, TX 75247

(214) 637-6282

Web site: http://www.nata.org/youthsports/index.htm

A professional association whose mission is to enhance the quality of health care provided by certified athletic trainers and advance the athletic training profession.

National Center for Sports Safety (NCSS)

2301 Morris Avenue, Suite 105

Birmingham, AL 35203

(205) 329-7535

Web site: http://www.sportssafety.org/
NCSS was founded to promote the importance of sports injury prevention and safety by developing and teaching sports safety classes and collecting and analyzing injury data.

National Youth Sports Safety Foundation (NYSSF)

One Beacon Street, Suite 3333

Boston, MA 02108

(617) 367-6677

Web site: http://www.nyssf.org
A non-profit organization dedicated to reducing the number and severity of youth's sports and fitness injuries, while promoting healthy development and in physical activity.

Web Sites

Due to the changing nature of Internet links, Rosen Publishing has developed an online list of Web sites related to the subject of this book. This site is updated regularly. Please use this link to access the list:

http://www.rosenlinks.com/faq/spin

Bernhardt, Gale. *Training Plans for Multisport Athletes* (Ultimate Training Series). Boulder, CO: VeloPress, 2000.

Cohen, Sasha, and Amanda Maciel. *Fire on Ice: Autobiography of a Champion Figure Skater.* New York, NY: HarperCollins Publishers, 2005.

Edelson, Edward. *Sports Medicine* (21st Century Health and Wellness). New York, NY: Chelsea House Publishers, 1999.

Hofstetter, Adam B. *Cool Careers Without College for People Who Love Sports* (Cool Careers Without College). New York, NY: Rosen Publishing, 2007.

Kaehler, Kathy. *Teenage Fitness: Get Fit, Look Good, and Feel Great!* New York, NY: HarperCollins, 2001.

Lee, Veronica. *Field Hockey* (Sports Injuries: How to Prevent, Diagnose, & Treat). Broomall, PA: Mason Crest Publishers, 2004.

Moe, Barbara. *Careers in Sports Medicine* (Career Resource Library). New York, NY: Rosen Publishing Group, 2002.

Shannon, Joyce Brennfleck. *Sports Injuries Information for Teens: Health Tips About Sports Injuries and Injury Prevention* (Teen Health Series). Detroit, MI: Omnigraphics, 2003.

About.com. "Sports Medicine: Concussion." Retrieved
September 2006 (http://sportsmedicine.about.com/cs/
head/a/concussion.htm).

American Academy of Orthopaedic Surgeons. "Achilles
Tendon." March 2001. Retrieved September 2006 (http://
orthoinfo.aaos.org/fact/thr_report.cfm?Thread_ID=124).

American Academy of Orthopaedic Surgeons. "Shin
Splints." February 2005. Retrieved September 2006
(http://orthoinfo.aaos.org/fact/thr_report.cfm?thread_
id=135&topcategory=Sports%20/%20Exercise).

American Academy of Orthopaedic Surgeons. "Stress
Fractures." March 2000. Retrieved September 2006
(http://orthoinfo.aaos.org/fact/thr_report.cfm?thread_
id=46&topcategory=sports).

Better Health Channel. "Bone Fractures—Treatment
Options." Retrieved September 2006 (http://www.
disability.vic.gov.au/bhcv2/bhcarticles.nsf/pages/Bone_
fractures_treatment_options?OpenDocument).

BUPA Health Information Team. "Tennis Elbow." January
2004. Retrieved October 2006 (http://hcd2.bupa.co.uk/
fact_sheets/html/tennis_elbow.html).

Children's Hospital Boston. "Sports Injury Statistics."
Retrieved October 2006 (http://www.childrenshospital.org/
az/Site1112/printerfriendlypageS1112P0.html).

Gorman, Christine. "To an Athlete, Aching Young." *Time.*
Vol. 168, No. 12. September 18, 2006.

Jenkins, Mark, MD. "Shin Splints." 2003. Retrieved October 2006
(http://www.rice.edu/~jenky/sports/shin.html).

Roberts, Robin. *Sports Injuries: How to Stay Safe and Keep on Playing.* Brookfield, CT: Millbrook Press, 2001.

U.S. Department of Health and Human Services, National Institutes of Health, National Institute of Arthritis and Musculoskeletal and Skin Diseases. "Handout on Health: Sports Injuries." April 2004. Retrieved September 2006 (http://www.niams.nih.gov/hi/topics/sports_injuries/Sports Injuries.htm#ra_2).

Index

Photo Credits

Cover, pp. 39 © www.istockphoto.com/Lisa F. Young; p. 5 © A. Ramey/PhotoEdit; p. 7 © www.shutterstock.com/Stephen Cobum; p. 10 © www.shutterstock.com/Shawn Pecor; p. 15 © www.shutterstock.com/Jack Dagley Photography; p. 13 © www. shutterstock.com/Galina Barskaya; pp. 20, 36, 46 © age fotostock/Superstock; p. 23 © Fotex/Custom Medical Stock Photo; p. 25 © Larry Mulvehill/Science Photo Library/Custom Medical Stock Photo; p. 28 © ISM/Phototake; p. 31 © Christopher Reeve Foundation; p. 33 © Howard C. Smith/Icon SMI; p. 38 © D Clarke Evans/NBAE/Getty Images; p. 43 © SIU Bio Med/ Custom Medical Stock Photo; p. 49 © www.istockphoto.com/ Jennifer Trenchard; p. 51 © AFP/Getty Images; p. 53 © Michael Newman/PhotoEdit; p. 54 © Mark Richards/PhotoEdit.

Designer: Evelyn Horovicz; **Photo Researcher:** Marty Levick